Blood Wolf Moon

## ALSO BY ELISE PASCHEN

### POETRY
*Houses: Coasts*
*Infidelities*
*Bestiary*
*The Nightlife*
*Tallchief* ᏦᎳᏂᎦ ᏐᎠ

### CO-EDITOR
*Poetry in Motion*
*Poetry in Motion from Coast to Coast*
*Poetry Speaks*
*Poetry Speaks Expanded*

### EDITOR
*Poetry Speaks to Children*
*Poetry Speaks Who I Am*
*The Eloquent Poem*

# Blood Wolf Moon

*poems*

ELISE PASCHEN

Red Hen Press | *Pasadena, CA*

*Blood Wolf Moon*
Copyright © 2025 by Elise Paschen
All Rights Reserved

No part of this book may be used or reproduced in any manner whatsoever without the prior written permission of both the publisher and the copyright owner.

Book design by Mark E. Cull

Library of Congress Cataloging-in-Publication Data

Names: Paschen, Elise, author.
Title: Blood wolf moon: poems / Elise Paschen.
Description: First edition. | Pasadena, CA: Red Hen Press, 2025.
Identifiers: LCCN 2024018736 (print) | LCCN 2024018737 (ebook) | ISBN 9781636282084 (trade paperback) | ISBN 9781636282398 (ebook)
Subjects: LCGFT: Poetry.
Classification: LCC PS3566.A77283 B56 2025 (print) | LCC PS3566.A77283 (ebook) | DDC 811/.54—dc23/eng/20240429
LC record available at https://lccn.loc.gov/2024018736
LC ebook record available at https://lccn.loc.gov/2024018737

The National Endowment for the Arts, the Los Angeles County Arts Commission, the Ahmanson Foundation, the Dwight Stuart Youth Fund, the Max Factor Family Foundation, the Pasadena Tournament of Roses Foundation, the Pasadena Arts & Culture Commission and the City of Pasadena Cultural Affairs Division, the City of Los Angeles Department of Cultural Affairs, the Audrey & Sydney Irmas Charitable Foundation, the Meta & George Rosenberg Foundation, the Albert and Elaine Borchard Foundation, the Adams Family Foundation, Amazon Literary Partnership, the Sam Francis Foundation, and the Mara W. Breech Foundation partially support Red Hen Press.

First Edition
Published by Red Hen Press
www.redhen.org

# Acknowledgments

Grateful acknowledgment is made to the editors of the following publications:

The Academy of American Poets Poem-a-Day: "Aerial, Wild Pine," "𐓏𐒰𐓓𐒰𐓓𐒷/Wahzhazhe/Osage"; *Action, Spectacle*: "Heritage XI" as "Heritage of the Blood Wolf Moon, XI"; *The Harvard Advocate*: "Ghost Fishing"; *Harvard Review*: "Heritage I & II"; *Hudson Review*: "Outside the Door"; *Indigenous Ecopoetry* (Green Linden Press): "Heritage IV & V"; *The Massachusetts Review*: "Heritage X"; *The New Yorker*: "Heritage III & IX"; *Orion*: "Lighthouse, Shipwreck"; *Poet Lore*: "*Lupine* Nocturne"; *Poetry*: "After *Killers of the Flower Moon*," "Heritage VI & VII" as "Heritage of the Blood Wolf Moon VI & VII," "Stationery," "Trot Song," and "Typewriter"; *Prairie Schooner*: "Heritage XIV"; *The Southampton Review*: "No"; *Vox Populi*: "*Dahlia* Aubade," "Letters"; *Water~stone Review*: "Divination"; *Yellow Medicine Review*: "Heritage XIII."

*Le Cinquieme Monde—Voix Amerindiennes* (*The Fifth World—Native American Voices*, 2024): "Heritage VIII," "Transatlantic," and "Triangles"; *The Last Milkweed* (Tupelo Press, 2024): "Sumac in Pawhuska"; *Living Nations, Living Words: An Anthology of First Peoples Poetry* (W.W. Norton, 2021): "Heritage X"; *Love Can Be: A Literary Collection about Our Animals* (Kirkpatrick, 2018): "Quarrel of Sparrows"; *Poetry Goes to the Movies* (Pacific Coast Poetry Series/Beyond Baroque Books, 2025): "After *Killers of the Flower Moon*"; *The Polaris Trilogy* (Brick Street Poetry, 2023): "Snare" as "Star"; *Stronger Than Fear* (Cave Moon Press, 2022): "Kitihawa"; *Wherever I'm At: An Anthology of Chicago Poetry* (After Hours Press, 2022): "Kitihawa."

"Heritage XII" as "Swan Queen" in Google Doodle Celebrating Maria Tallchief, November 14, 2020; "Heritage X" featured in *Living Nations, Living Words: A Map of First Peoples Poetry* at the Library of Congress, created by U.S. Poet Laureate Joy Harjo, 2020; "Kitihawa Speaks" as "Kitihawa" featured in the 2019 *Floating Museum* art installation called "Founders," honoring Kitihawa (Potawatomi) and her husband Jean Baptiste Point Du Sable; "Distant" appeared in a photographic diptych by Keli Mashburn and exhibited in *Creativity 2020* at the Osage Nation Museum; "Distant" made into a short film, *Distant*, by Mashburn and premiered at the UCLA Native Film Festival, 2022.

"Heritage VII, X & XII" in *Tallchief 𐓄𐓘𐓧𐓣𐓤𐒻 𐒷𐓟𐒰* (Magic City Books Press, 2023).

With gratitude to: Tree Swenson, Christian Campbell, Joy Harjo, Cynthia Atkins, Grace Schulman, Dana Gioia, Sophie Cabot Black, Rachel DeWoskin, Thea Goodman, Gabriel Fried, Ruben Quesada, Julie Parson Nesbitt, Lisa Lee, Larry Kaplan, Jean Hanff Korelitz, Gordon Henry, Heid E. Erdrich, Kimberly Blaeser, Ellen Rachlin, David Kuhn, Bill Wadsworth, Jen Levine, Daryl Hannah, Suzin Farber, Jackie Skibine, Chief Geoffrey Standing Bear, Cecelia Tallchief, Jan Tallchief, Brandy Lemon, Johnna Johnson, Cindy Groce, Thomas Tallchief, Dana Bear, Jordan Poorman Cocker, Wilson Pipestem, Veronica Pipestem, Moira Redcorn, Marla Redcorn Miller, Shannon Shaw Duty, Chad Renfro, Addie Roanhorse, TL Salisbury, Keli Mashburn, Lily Gladstone, Russ Tallchief. Love always to Stuart, Alexandra, and Stephen.

Thank you, Kate Gale and Mark Cull, and the remarkable staff at Red Hen Press, especially Rebeccah Sanhueza and Monica Fernandez.

*Dedicated to*

Eliza Bigheart Tall Chief (1870–1962)

Ruth Porter Tallchief (1899–1981)

Maria Tallchief Paschen (1925–2013)

# Contents

## I

| | |
|---|---|
| Heritage | 15 |

## II

| | |
|---|---|
| *Lupine* Nocturne | 37 |
| Lighthouse, Shipwreck | 38 |
| Ghost Fishing | 39 |
| Aerial, *Wild Pine* | 40 |
| *Dahlia* Aubade | 42 |
| Quarrel of Sparrows | 43 |
| Distant | 44 |
| *No* | 45 |
| Kitihawa Speaks | 46 |

## III

| | |
|---|---|
| The Terrors | 49 |
| In Memoriam | 50 |
| After *Killers of the Flower Moon* | 51 |

## IV

| | |
|---|---|
| *Transatlantic* | 55 |
| Triangles | 58 |
| 123 West 69th Street | 60 |
| Ode to the Lost Mother | 64 |
| What Warning | 65 |
| Outside the Door | 67 |
| Poison Tree | 68 |

## V

| | |
|---|---|
| 𐓇𐓇𐓘𐓓𐓘𐓓𐓘 / *Wahzhazhe* / Osage | 71 |
| Sumac in Pawhuska | 72 |
| Trot Song | 73 |
| Peyote Button Necklace | 75 |
| Letters | 77 |
| Divination | 78 |
| Skywriting | 79 |
| 𐓂𐓪𐓘𐓲𐓇 / *Ho'-e-ga* / Snare | 80 |
| 𐓇𐓇𐓘𐓬𐓘𐓓𐓘 / *Waléze* / Stationery | 81 |
| 𐓨𐓘𐓓𐓘 𐓐𐓘𐓬𐓘𐓓𐓘 / *Mą́ze Htáhtaze* / Typewriter | 82 |

Notes     85

*To the door of the House of Mystery I have come.*

from an Osage song

I

# Heritage

## I

                                    Once I had a name
for everything I possessed, but now am silent, afraid
                       to trespass. When I leave the conversation,
     or seem preoccupied, I travel that island
                          where lupines in summer devour
the rocky terrain, those flowers named
                after the slate blue wolves who keen
   in night's hollow, who scavenge
                             the tundra, across the hectares
and hectares, the way they test
                the air, how their topaz eyes never lose sight
   of their quarry, how they track
                      any escape with a slow nod,
a careful paw to the earth. Those wolves
                       never roved that island. I only pretend they did.
   Stories of those who came before:
                          the ones who followed the *cloudy gray*—
*the loafer wolves* or *buffalo runners*—across the plains,
                chanted their songs, hunting, haunted,
      found their shapes, carved
                      silhouettes in the sky, those whose land
extended past states, the extinct,
                extinguished, our next of kin.

## II

        Extinguished, our next of kin
descended from constellations,
          *The Little Ones,* desiring a form,
   out of air into muscle, sinew, limbs,
  landing in red oak trees,
       and, with the heft of their new
bodies, scattered capped oak-nuts
          across the earth. Underneath
    branches—each acorn, a child to be born.
  How Eagle navigated
       the downward flight, wings
spackled, catching spirals
         of wind. Waters blown across land masses
    sculpted by Great Elk, the *Earth Maker,*
  as hooves sunk, torso
     and antlers heaved into ocean.
*The Water People, The Name Givers,*
        gave appellations to
   *The Sky People, The Land People.*
  I have always been
     earth-bound and obstinate,
drawn to these rising and falling hills,
       the tallgrass prairies, the *Deer*
   *Rutting Moon* hovering over the ridge.
  How I mapped the rental car
     onto backroads—the trails my relatives
crisscrossed on their seasonal hunts—
       until I was lost. My Osage name
    𐓏𐒰𐓐𐓂𐓇𐒼𐒰𐓘
  descends from the Buffalo clan.

                          I seek out bodies of water,
the way those who came before
                                         settled along the deep tributaries,
                  the veins on the backs
     of our hands, hands I recognize
                       in those oval family portraits—long,
lean, poised. I was
             born in the month of the Blood Wolf Moon.

## III

I was born in the month of the Blood Wolf Moon.
         My mother said icicles shook the trees
   as she and my father traipsed
     along the black sheet sidewalk
          to their convertible. Her timed contractions
stretched out, hours long, until almost midnight.
       After how many miscarriages.
   Hospital bedside, my aunt and uncle
     smiled over the crib. Or was that just
        a photograph? Tell me
about departure. Tell me
        how often she left the newborn, jetted
   away on Pan Am, tied up the ribbons
    of her satin toe shoes.
         I am not one to antagonize her.
I bow low to her voice. She who crossed
        the Iron Curtain, searching for the baby
   photos inside stamped envelopes.
     Memory's sleight of hand.
        I don't remember how she vanished,
or when, tiptoeing into the cape
       of night, wrapped in ermine, in mink,
  flabbergasting audiences
     with every pirouette. Frozen, perfect,
        the star blazing onstage.

## IV

                            The star, blazing on the stage
of the firmament, the brightest of stars,
                            *Sirius*, the *Dog Star*,
        flashy shiner in the constellation
*Canis Major*. Named *The Trickster*
                        by the Pawnee or *The Coyote Star*.
The Osage said *The Wolf that Hangs by the Side*
                            *of Heaven Star*, alone, compact, content
             to howl louder than any other.
   One night I heard the wolves
                      inside their makeshift enclosure,
yowling back to the sirens.
                          Our two dogs strained
        on the leash. The caterwauling
   of wolves carried by wind
                    across blocks of tree-thick
streets. The rough blasts in this city.
                          The maelstroms on that lupine
        island when I couldn't
   hear my voice shout,
                  warning our children.

From Pawhuska to Fairfax—
                          driving in Oklahoma—
     how brash, the wind.

## V

                                                  How brash the wind
on Highway 60 that powers
                                                        colossal creatures stalking
                  the landscape. Some call the wind turbines
     eye sores, others miss the silhouettes
                           of oil derricks. I have read
the Osage never owned their own
                                  oil companies, leasing the land
                to others—Phillips Petroleum,
     Standard. Fortunes amassed.
                        Because of headrights from that mineral
underground, her father,
                     my mother said, never worked
        a day in his life—cruising the golf courses,
   tracking pheasant. Her Scots-Irish
                mother pushed to move
their young family away from the oil
                     boom town riddled with crime.
           In their maroon Pierce-
  Arrow my grandparents drove across
               the country, settling in Beverly Hills.
Every day my grandmother shepherded
                       the girls to ballet class. In grammar school
           children chased the two sisters
  down hallways, whooped war cries,
               demanding to see their feathers.
*Is your last name "Tall"*
                       *or "Chief"?* The Osage
      girls were bullied
because of their last name.

## VI

                    Because of their last name,
the sisters believed they owned
                          the town. ***TALL CHIEF*** spelled
          out on the marquee,
     the gem of Fairfax,
               built by their father.
That theater, a shell,
                    as long as I can
        recall, a shell
     emptied from inside,
                without nacre or mussel.
Ghosts of dressing rooms
                  beneath the sweep of stage,
        the place where vaudevillians,
    between the acts, swapped out
              their costumes. Last spring's
tornado, tore up the town,
                  now an abandoned
       movie set, businesses boarded
    up, except the dollar
            store at the end of Main.
I step across the glass
                like cracked ice, outside
       the blownout storefronts, the beams
   of the theater's roof, newly-
         refurbished, blasted away.
As if trying to rewrite
               an ending, we climb
     the hill to excavate the terracotta house,
   my mother's childhood home.

## VII

My mother's childhood home
where the driveway is overgrown
with weeds, surrounded by upstart trees,
sycamores and oaks, tunneling
uphill toward the brick edifice.
A carrion beetle, bright orange
and black, scuttles across
the path. The endangered
*Burying Beetle* digs a grave,
mummifies its prey—
the voles and snakes—then returns
to the tomb to mate
and raise its young.
If discovered on a construction
site in Oklahoma, all drilling
terminates. A shred of white
curtain in an upstairs window—
I imagine my grandmother still alive,
inside the ruined house.
My grandmother's fudge
cools on the wooden kitchen
table downstairs. In the basement
a rattler twines inside
the dryer. Outside, I cut
cattle on quarter
horses, pressing my twelve-year-old
knees into leather, swerving in sync
with the herd. Riding back
to the barn, the horse
is spooked. A garter snake ripples
beneath a plot of leaves.

## VIII

         Beneath a plot of leaves
lie the bones of ancestors
            buried in earthen mounds,
     hillocks built along the bluffs
  of rivers. Strong rains pillaged
         the dirt, loosed from holy
burial ground—mandible, femur,
           clavicle. How to warn
      generations of mourners whose tears
  wet new graves. How to renew
         the rites of passage, placing earth
on foreheads. Weep and pray.
           There was a name
     for someone who desecrated
  tombs, who crossed
         the divide between man
and wolf, running
           on all fours. Two decades
     ago, an amusement
   park owner dug up
        these mounds in Missouri
to construct a sky lift.
            The "inconvenience" of burial chambers.
    Scavenger, werewolf:
all for the sake of a dime.

## IX

                                For the sake of a dime,
oblivious owners invented
                                                           names for teams: *Braves,*
                        *Chiefs, Redskins.* Football
           zealots, my parents
                             rooted for the *Bears.* Last night,
someone holding a glass
                                              of Sancerre at a posh
                     French restaurant said,
        "Why should they care
                        about the name *Redskins*?
Why make such a fuss?"
                                      My blond hair
               fooled her. Our host whispered,
        "Her family is Osage."
                        After we pushed back
chairs, during goodbyes,
                                      she apologized.

                   When my mother, Maria
         Tallchief, danced the muse
                       Terpsichore in *Apollo*
on the stage of the Paris
                                     Opera House, the audience
                embraced her, shouting,
        "Encore! Encore!"
                     The headlines of '47 read
*"Peau Rouge Danse a l'Opera."*
                                   *Peau Rouge*, Red Skin,
              a phrase she learned

        to ignore. Reading my friend's
                      manuscript, I'm stunned
to discover the origin
                                of Red Skins—*the bodies*
        *of Natives brought in for bounty.*


      During my youth,
                  every Sunday in the fall,
my parents bicycled
                                along Lake Michigan
            to cheer their home
     team playing in Soldier
                Field, a stadium named
as a memorial to those who died
                                in combat, constructed
          the year my mother was born.

## X

                                    The year my mother was born
in Fairfax, Oklahoma,
                                          white men were marrying Osage
               women and killing them
      for their headrights.
                                 My mother was born a year after
The Indian Citizenship Act was passed—
                                       Indians tied to the US
                 for or against their wills.
        Three years before her birth, her half-sister
                                Baby Ruth's grave was dynamited
with nitroglycerine by outlaws
                                         scavenging for diamonds
             and gold buried inside the casket.
       In the Tallchief plot
                           I wander through family history—
the marble monuments,
                                angelic statues—measuring
                each step on grass,
    memorizing photographs.
                          This one of a striking
beauty, my great grandmother
                                  Eliza Bigheart Tall Chief, 1870–1962,
              surviving her husband
      by fifty years. The widow, the adored
                          grandmother of my mother. Eliza.
Only now do I see my name
                      a permutation of hers.

              At home in Chicago
     every day I pass
                   family photographs framed

on walls. My great grandfather's
                                        oval sepia portrait
                        of his boyish face
    replicated on the headstone.
                                Instead of the young bride,
here is Eliza, a tribal elder,
                                        wrapped in a multi-colored
                blanket, standing outside
        her front porch, a photo
                                taken after all those years
                she outlived him.

## XI

                                          She outlived him,
my mother dying
                                                                                     nine years after my father.
                                The tomb my mother
            inhabited that first year, lying
                                        on the suede beige couch,
sealed by the dark,
                                                                       black-out curtains pulled tight,
                            blocking the changing trees
        whose seasons my blue-eyed
                                father followed, shut out
the backdrop of lake
                                                           beyond the bluff. My father,
                      amateur limnologist, walked
           the pebbled beach each
                                       morning, tried to keep
his strip of sand safe
                                                                from erosion, building
                        breakwaters, constructing barrier
          boulders. During my childhood
                                  summers of their separation,
we helped him dig holes
                                                      in sand, to bury deep
                     the tide of alewives. The stench
        of those fish, their silver bodies,
                          shriveled in the sun. Our dog
loved to roll among the carcasses.
                                                   We splashed my playful
                  father in the azure-cold
     lake, the infinite lake
                        masquerading as ocean.

## XII

                                          Masquerading as ocean,
the duplicitous waves:
                                                  *Beware the undertow.*
                       Across a lake my mother
     floated, a swan,
                              spell-bound by day, transformed
back to human at night.
                                    As a child, with every
              shift of vibrato, I could
     predict the enchantment.
                              Let me tell you about
a procession of swans,
                                       the swish of waves
               luring beyond the stage.
     After encores,
                           my mother's face
shone when she saw
                                     my eagerness, curtained
            behind the wings, her only
     child, a fairy
                        tale made flesh.
Her moonlit face
                                   encompassed by ivory
          swan feathers.

## XIII

            Encompassed by swan feathers,
her face lights up the screen:
              *Remembering Maria Tallchief.*
        A mother I can't remember
before her dementia.
            I've been tagged. A photo
diptych: Swan Queen
              side by side
          Princess of the Osage Nation
    the day she was named
          ᏏᏂᏣᏰ-ᏥᎣᏧᏁ

*Two Standards.*
              The photographer caught
         her in the act of fastening
    buckskin cords of her ceremonial
            headdress, a corolla
of white-tufted eagle plumes
              she wears as if
         it's every day. In the background
    oil derricks and bluegrass
           prairie. How young
she looks. On her wrist a gold
             bracelet I safeguard,
        concealed in a drawer.
    A string of pearls around
           her neck. Luminous orchid pinned
to her black dress. A watch
              I don't recognize. On her wedding
      finger a band from her

          short-lived second
                              marriage before she
met the sky-blue gaze
                                      of my father, her final
                   husband. Always
        a name change.

## XIV

            Always a name change:
*People of the Middle Waters,*
              the tribe known as *Ni-u-kon-ska,*
       was called Osage
    by French fur trappers.
          American traders, exchanging brass
pots for beaver pelts,
           misheard the pronunciation,
      anglicizing the name.
   Middle Waters, junction
         of the great rivers: Missouri,
Ohio, Mississippi, Tennessee,
          Wabash, Arkansas
     and Illinois flooding the mouth
  of the Osage River. Now
        ᔕᴧᗱᴧᗱɑ
*Wahzhazhe.* Osage.
          After marrying,
     I never altered
  mine. My mother, once
       she retired and returned
to my father, took
          pride in signing Mrs.
     Paschen. If I could,
   I'd change my middle
        name, Maria, her stage
name, to Tallchief.
         Tall Chief once known as
*Kid He Kah Stah Tsa*
  ƙᴧᴝnƙɑ ᴄᴈɑ.

How some beings evolve
into their appellations,
that evolution from wolf
to dog: a puppy newly
discovered frozen
in Siberian permafrost,
18,000 years old.
In childhood, I was saved
by a dog I called
my own. Now
I have a name

ZAZA ARÑA

II

## *Lupine* Nocturne

Ranks of purple bloom invade.
The plant, named *wolf*, devours
dirt and silt and loam. On this island
it's constant dusk. Lose track of hours.

The name, from *wolf*, devours
a bullseye moon, quixotic sun.
Constant dusk turns minutes to hours
while speech grows slow like black pearl sand.

A bullseye moon, quixotic sun
muscle for place, take out the sky.
My speech grows slow, the grit of sand.
So hard to sleep in wolfsbane light.

Dirt and silt and loam on this island.
I cannot sleep. It's always light.
The ranks of purple bloom invade—
with every spike, take out the sky.

## Lighthouse, Shipwreck

I track what's absent—
faint apparition
of landing poles
where cormorants
congregate. Low tide.

Sidewheel steamers,
a century ago,
docked off this spit
of sand, taking shelter
at Pilots Landing.

Newcomers climbed
the burnt copper
cliffs to the far-off
lighthouse, muslin skirts
spilling like cream.

Pale honey-suckle
sentinels flank
the sloping road.
Inhaling summer
sweet, I recall

boulders of islands
and the myth of whales
bashed against rocks,
staining the clay
a blood-red dusk.

All that we've lost,
those deserting us,
the flame once coaxed,
stark Indian markers,
that lighthouse beam.

# Ghost Fishing

Along this coast every boulder repeats a story:
a wife implored her husband, out of earshot,

"Don't leave me stranded at the ocean's edge."
The trout bundle on her back slowed her down.

I lose track of mine as the winds pick up.
Witnessing the sun at daybreak, she turned to stone.

The fishermen threw dice of walrus teeth. Snake Eyes.
Last night, by a fire, I lost every round.

Inside the rock, spirits bellow to escape.
Like herds of stallions, waves stampede the shore.

Buffeted by high winds, I hear his shout,
while beneath, shoals of quick fish ghost the depth.

## Aerial, *Wild Pine*

A flare of russet,
green fronds, surprise
of flush against
the bare gray cypress
in winter woods.

*Cardinal wild pine,
quill-leaf airplant*
or *dog-drink-water.*
Spikes of bright bloom—
exotic plumage.

How they contour
against the trunk.
I miss that closeness
against my skin,
milky expression.

Before they latched,
their grief revealed
in such a flash.
Seekers of light,
poised acrobats.

Over the wetlands
a *snail kite* skims
tallgrass, then swoops
to scoop the *apple
snail* in curved bill.

The provenance
of names, of raptor
and prey, the beak,
like a trap door,
unhinging flesh.

The way two beings
create a space
for one another—
the bud to branch,
tongue against nipple.

## *Dahlia* Aubade

*Devil star*
*Fear to die*

Growing here
In the crook

Of a sleeve
The blue note

Each one tolls
Heavenward

Sky anthem
Root to slip

Knot of rope
Bell so clear

Wake up now
Cut your want

You uproot
Tuber bloom

## Quarrel of Sparrows

When I take flight
far from the house—

lonely for choirs,
riotous in trees—

a visitation
of wings, whirs, arcs

in sky, then lights
on city sidewalk.

How they survive
winter, back-alley

scrappers, who worry
feeders for millet,

sunflower seeds,
bicker for hours,

while my boots plod
across brick driveway

in January,
crunching the snow.

I track the bright
dash of their chatter,

while the crisscrossing
of wings will shadow

across my day
into the night,

such brazen pluck
soldiering the storm.

Adrift in the house,
we'll sleep while staunch

house sparrows huddle
together guarded

against the white.
Flurries inside—

their fury dies.
The snow won't stop.

## Distant

In dreams I walk through crowds,
Brushing arms, knocking elbows.
Skin to skin: hands are bare.

Crocuses congregate
in beds, along sidewalks.
Unlatching city gates,

I breathe each stranger's breath,
as if a new-cut bloom,
unafraid of anyone.

I walk through every crowd,

not shunned by anyone.
Each scent, a new-cut bloom.
I breathe each stranger's breath,

unlatching city gates.
In beds along sidewalks,
crocuses congregate.

## *No*

Across the table from you both,
with the Mediterranean
Sea Bass splayed-out across the plate,

at the hip Brooklyn restaurant,
my college best friend and you,
married almost twenty-eight years—

shared stories about parenthood
and our own youth, the indiscretions
of concealed bottles, sneaking liquor

from glass shelves in our parents' bars.
Then the talk turned to our young sons.
You said that boys must learn that *No*

*means No*, later remembering
a conversation in our twenties.
Driving up-island I had said,

"Is it wrong for a woman
to say *no*?" You wondered then why
I had been raised to just obey?

Back home I witness citizens
repeating *no*, while every day
this brute in charge ignores our words,

like the man I couldn't fight off
that night he squeaked open the door
and, wordless, crawled into my bed.

45

## Kitihawa Speaks

My relatives guide fur traders between swamp
and bog, down age-old trails, under pine trees
and black oaks, navigating the tributaries,
the sweeps and turns. My husband and I

followed the river to its mouth, this spot
where the sun and the moon climb above
the rim of lake. I feed the traders hot
loaves from our Bakery, milk crocks from our Dairy.

Silent as fog rising from the marsh, I observe.
The traders barter canoes for our whitewood dugouts.
My husband broods at the prow of the long table,
candles sputtering, reflected between two mirrors.

Clearing the wooden plates, I question the way they shake hands.
I see blazing greed, our earth parched, my descendants gone.

III

## The Terrors

A man stands with a gun beside my bed about to shoot. At the door of my bedroom, at the top of the stairs, I wake up. Somewhere in the house men plot my murder. I escape death night after night.

The dreams surface from your inherited past, a friend suggests. If your grandmother's sister drowned, then a fear of water would be passed down generation after generation.

My grandmother never spoke about the gunshots, the poisonings, the house blown up down the street in Fairfax. She was young, raising three small children.

My mother told me her cousin Pearl Bigheart's father was murdered during the Reign of Terror. People still are afraid to talk about it.

Decades later, my grandmother's dog, poisoned by neighbors, dragged himself up her back steps to die.

# In Memoriam

*George Bigheart*
*Born September 12, 1876*
*Died June 29, 1923*

George Bigheart, 46 years old, of Grayhorse, died Friday at an Oklahoma City hospital. He is survived by his daughter, Pearl Bigheart.

On June 28, 1923, William Hale and Bryan Burkhart put George Bigheart on a train to Oklahoma City to be taken to a hospital. There, doctors suspected that he had ingested poisoned whiskey. Bigheart called his attorney W.W. Vaughan of Pawhuska, asking him to come to the hospital as soon as possible for an urgent meeting. Vaughan complied and went to Oklahoma City. Bigheart had said he had suspicions about who was behind the murders and had access to incriminating documents that would prove his claims.

Vaughan boarded a train that night to return to Pawhuska but was missing the next morning when the Pullman porter went to wake him. Vaughan's body was later found beside the railroad tracks near Pershing, about five miles south of Pawhuska. Bigheart died at the hospital that same morning. The documents that Bigheart gave to Vaughan were not found.

### After *Killers of the Flower Moon*

Lily Gladstone confides she wore my great
grandmother Eliza's blankets in three scenes.

I don't remember my great grandmother, though
in a photo, aged ninety, she holds me in her arms.

The actress plays Mollie Burkhart, who lived
down the street from Eliza in Fairfax.

Hands out wide, Lily says Eliza had a *broad wingspan*.
She pleated the wool broadcloth several times.

Through an open window, wings outstretched, an eagle
owl looms toward Mollie's mother, dying from poison.

My mother told me that owls in trees wailed
the windswept night before her father died.

Wrapping my great grandmother's striped blanket
around her shoulders, Mollie asks her husband,

during a downpour, not to close the window.
*Be still*, she says, *and listen to the rain*.

Eliza's blankets fold and unfold stories.
Into every pattern, I fly back home.

The Osage replaced hide robes with Dutch-
traded blankets in the mid-19th century.

I stop breathing during the night of film
when a murderer calls Osage women *blankets*.

While her husband injects Mollie with arsenic,
each sister is shot, poisoned, or bombed to death.

A woman, in a voice-over, foreshadows,
*this blanket is a target on our backs.*

In the quiet, after Mollie's obituary
is reported, I only hear rain.

Outside the theater, silent thunderbirds
overhead spread dark cloud-spattered wings,

outlining circles across a broadcloth.
Inside each target, a hole in the sky.

IV

*Transatlantic*

## Flight

In the blue hour, before take-off, my mother smells like *L'Heure Bleue*. Inside her sleeve I bury my nose to block the fumes. My red coat and hat match, and the patent leather shoes squeak. This will be a long flight across the Atlantic. My mother says, *Go to sleep*. I sleep, my head cradled in my mother's lap.

## Arrival and Departure

At the Orly gate, my uncle and aunt strike dramatic poses. In his arms, my uncle balances red roses, handing them to my mother. Dressed in a black suit and high heels, Hermès clutch in hand, she takes long strides. Everyone looks at her.

Driving to Sèvres in my uncle's Peugeot, my aunt says, "Remember that incredible young Russian boy I wrote you about—the one who danced Blue Bird in *Sleeping Beauty*? You said you were looking for a new partner. Maybe he's the one."

As drizzle falls on the suburbs of Paris, my mother stares out the window. I imagine blue birds, snuggle close to her.

## Sèvres

Blue dahlias border the garden. The calico cat Minouche runs away, disappears under a honeysuckle bush. I crawl after him, reaching out. With claws, he scratches the top of my hand, leaves pinpricks of blood. Soeur Ruth tells me not to cry. My mother kisses my hand, carries me upstairs to the bathroom where she washes the skin, iodines, adheres a Band-Aid.

# Triangles

                                            At the Normandy Hotel
in Deauville: my two-year-old
                                                        self grasps the reins
                    of a pony cart, and below
       stretches out arms
                             in calisthenics class
near the surf.
                                                  But then I turn
                the page and another
       photo takes me
                          by surprise. The famous
dancer, wearing
                                             a red sweater, legs
                outstretched in the sand,
       sitting beside a navy-
                  blue cabana, laughing.

That summer, after
                                            my mother leaves
                my father, she falls
       in love with Rudy,
                        a *Russki Malchick*.
She flies with him
                                          to Cologne, sending
                me away by train
       with Soeur Ruth to
                        St. Gallen and her family.
Several weeks later,
                                      we rejoin my
                mother in Copenhagen.
          On the paisley
                          Turkish rug of the pensionne,

Rudy regales me
                                                            with fables in broken
                        English, while on
       stage, my mother
                                        dances a *pas de deux*
with Erik in the tragic
                                                    ballet, *Miss Julie.*
                   Rudy leaves
        my mother for
                                Erik. I board
a plane bound for
                                                    Chicago with Soeur
                    Ruth. My mother
       presses the rose
                                in a book, returns
to New York to unpack
                                                        her suitcase alone.

## 123 West 69th Street

Over breakfast on Madison Avenue, I meet my mother's ghostwriter. It's a cold spring day. He had interviewed Betty Cage, who shared the bottom half of the brownstone near Lincoln Center with my mother. Betty said my mother left me for months alone with a young dancer who threw party after party. She worried about a five-year-old living upstairs in that house.

All these years later, why do I still wake up afraid there is a strange man in my room.

The ghostwriter suggests I call that irresponsible babysitter, still alive, and ask what happened.

I'm afraid to pick up the phone and hear what she will say.

# Ode to the Lost Mother

Where were you?

# What Warning

Ring the brass doorbell and then pound
with furious momentum and heft.

A black-eyed fly balances on the urn
five feet below the balustrade.

The cement sidewalk floods with earthworms
after the rain. What warning do they sing?

A scent of snuffed-out candles, smoke,
after the dream, wakes her up.

Watching the mother fling magic on TV,
she pictures moving to another state.

The soles leave impressions with every step.
"*What can't be explained,*" say the stairs.

Another night with the volume turned high.
Lightning outside. When will it crack?

The cement sidewalk floods with earthworms.
She pictures moving to another state.

A black-eyed fly balances on an urn.
After the dream, wakes her up.

*Ring the brass doorbell and then ask
what can't be explained*, say the stairs.

Five feet below the balustrade,
the soles leave impressions with every step's

ascent. Snuffed-out candles smoke
with furious momentum and heft.

After the rain, what warning do they sing?
Lightning outside, when will it crack.

She watches the mother on TV,
another night with the volume turned high.

## Outside the Door

I am the hairbrush,
bristles face-down, the mother
left behind on the bureau
with one dark strand of hair,
the hair she would pull back
into a horse's tail
at the nape of her neck.

I am the mirror
on the mother's vanity
in the bathroom upstairs
where uninvited guests
line up rows of white powder
while the teen babysitter
knocks, begging them to leave.

I am the lamp
beside the bed the child
switches on, hearing noises
outside her door, the floral
lamp, illuminating
fairy-tale books, someone
clicks off, flooding the dark.

## Poison Tree

A blood-red X marks the manchineel of ache.
*Little apples of death*, quick meals of ache.

An only child, I disappeared behind the page.
My mother mastered shadows to conceal the ache.

Avoid touching leaves, flowers, milky sap.
Is dangerous beauty a surreal ache?

Clouds, white-crested waves, surge. Droplets sting.
I harbor beneath a poison tree of ache.

For open wounds, my mother dabbed iodine.
*Salt air*, she said, *will heal the ache*.

Across the endless stage, red roses scatter,
alive with thorns. Strange passion, steal the ache.

v

𐓄𐓘𐓻𐓘𐓻𐓘 / *Wahzhazhe* / Osage

                                          The first language

𐓄𐓘𐓻𐓘𐓻𐓘 which Eliza,

                                                               her grandmother, spoke.

           the words 𐓎𐓘

                            I try to learn

                                        from a book, a dictionary.

What was my mother taught

                                                    as a young girl sitting

                       on the front stoop

        of her grandma's house

                                         inhabited by half-brothers

she revered. Her favorite,

                                               Hunky, hand outstretched,

                      showed her how to catch

           the wild horse

                              𐓊𐓈𐓄𐓈 𐓄𐓈𐓆𐓘𐓌𐓎

unbridled in the pasture.

                                               She knotted a paisley

                     bandana around her

          neck. This language

                             for throat 𐓆𐓂𐓆𐓘

and tongue 𐓏𐓘𐓋𐓘—

                                             words she learns

                     to speak but then

                           𐓄𐓘𐓏𐓎 the rope

          forgets. She loosens

from the horse's crest.

## Sumac in Pawhuska

*ákahamį žúuce dée, pée duuštáke hta de?*
*Who is going to undress that one with the red coat?*
    From the *Osage Dictionary* by Carolyn Quintero

Against black jacks,
                    the wedding coat
                                        red of sumac
flares bright, soon
                    to be stripped
                                        bare. The tires
drum a trot
                    rhythm through
                                        the tall-grass prairie,
a horse-raiding
                    song, centuries old.
                                        Dried-up stalks,
ghosts of sunflowers,
                    bow down in fields.
                                        During the Drum
Ceremony, a wife
                    will bestow her wedding
                                        coat, the one handed
down through her family,
                    once a soldier's. What
                                        can I release
from this mortal heart?
                    A red-tailed hawk
                                        alights in a cedar.
Come wildfire
                    season, those trees
                                        will explode.

## Trot Song

During the Grayhorse

        Dances in June,

                my mother side-stepped

around the circle,

        echoing moves

                her grandmother

Tallchief had taught.

        Someone pulled me

                aside, insisting

I stop my mother

        from dancing. When

                she had to lie

motionless during

        an MRI,

                my mother said

she would pretend

        to hear the drum

                pulse of her youth.


My daughter and I

        now enter the circle,

                pick up our pace

as we imitate

        the gait of mares

                trotting, those songs

chanted by

        generations

                of warriors

who galloped back

        into the heart

                of the village.

Wrapped in what

        we inherited,

                striped broadcloth blankets,

    we shadow chestnuts,

                  pintos, palominos,

                                      claiming back hoofbeat.

## Peyote Button Necklace

                                                      Because of Indian Boarding
School, my cousin says,
                                                                 our grandfather only
                     spoke English though
           his mother communicated
                                  in *wahzhazhe* 𐓇𐓣𐓻𐓣𐓻𐓜.
Conditioned by Boarding
                                                 School, my cousin
                        thinks our grandfather
             was convinced to marry
                            outside the tribe.
Why, I say,
                                          I need to study
                 our heritage
         in books. My mother
                            confided, when she
was a child, her Osage
                                        grandmother would sneak
                    her into covert Peyote
          gatherings, hidden in
                           hollows, beneath the moon.


                   My mother's beaded
       Peyote button
                       necklace, symbol
of the Native American
                                Church, worn by her
                  grandmother to those
          sacred rites, dangles
                         from a floor-lamp
beside my writing
                                desk. Like a flower,
               upside down,

                    a red bloom bursts

                                                    against tiny green
trade beads. Cowrie

                                                      shells chant into
                              the prayer of night.

## Letters

*Ruby-Throated*, she
undaunted, taps the porch screen,
types tiny missives.

# Divination

Snowbound, a round
                of Robins huddle
                                on high. Ruby-

red baubles, they
                garland icy
                                branches of the oak,

hiding song
                inside. I forecast
                                birth, a steady

melt when nests
                empty for months
                                beneath rain

pipes, shingles
                will be feathered,
                                twined: those clutches

of three, their own
                trinity, after
                                the tug of worms

from mud, beneath
                the puff of wing,
                                miniscule eggs,

bluer than rapture.

## Skywriting

Whistles, trills

        distract my sense

                of line. Splotches

        of chants, ink

blots scrawl what

        messages in air.

                *Pine Siskin*, *Nuthatch*,

        *Cedar Waxwing* toss

bright notes I

        try to write

                while *Black-capped*

        *Chickadees* clutch

stripped maple

        branches and spy

                into this glass

        aviary. They banter

as I translate.

        My wing-flutter

                shatters the divide.

## 𐓏𐓘𐓬𐓤𐓣 / *Ho'-e-ga* / Snare

| | | |
|---|---|---|
| 𐓏𐓎𐓷𐓣𐓏𐓣 | *hu-xiⁿ-ha* | Fish scales |
| 𐓼𐓎𐓬𐓲𐓬𐓲𐓷𐓘 | *thi-bthu'-bthu-xe* | tremble |
| 𐓒𐓎 𐓤𐓃𐓏𐓣 | *ni-ko-ha* | at the edge of the water, |
| 𐓒𐓎 𐓃𐓯𐓃𐓺𐓘 | *ni o-sho'dse* | smoky with mud. |
| 𐓎𐓒𐓄𐓘𐓏𐓎 𐓺'𐓘 | *Noⁿ-pe'-hi ts'e* | Starved, |
| 𐓒𐓎𐓃𐓟𐓘𐓬𐓣𐓎 | *niu'-moⁿ-bthiⁿ*— | I walk in the water. |
| 𐓟𐓘𐓤𐓏 𐓛𐓤𐓣 | *mąhka saakí* | Blazing star, |
| 𐓏𐓃 𐓬𐓣 | *ho-çoⁿ* | braided fish, |
| 𐓁𐓤𐓃𐓘 | *u-bthiⁿ-ge* | I catch |
| 𐓏𐓘𐓬𐓤𐓣 | *ho'-e-ga* | in the snare of life. |
| 𐓷𐓎𐓲𐓄𐓘 | *wáaspe* | Stay quiet, |
| 𐓼𐓣 | *žą́ą́* | stay all night. |

## ᏍᎵᏣᏃᎠ / *Waléze* / Stationery

| | | |
|---|---|---|
| ńƙusᏞᎧ | íkuspa | Sign with a thumbprint |
| ɢƙóᏞᎠ | škópe | deep |
| ᒼӑɮᎧ | májhka | in this earth. |
| ᎠӧꙄᎠ | tóoce | The throat, |
| ҺoӑǴ | xoé | like a waterfall, rumbles. |
| ᏍᎵᏣᎠᎯᎫ | waséhtahü | A sycamore's |
| ɮōᎠҺᎠ | hkeetáxe | shadow |
| ҺᎴɢꙄÚᏌ | ðaašcúe | swallows |
| ᒼńѰᎵᏕҺᎴ | míraska | the swan. |
| ᏞōᎫóᎠᎴ | lǫǫhóohtą | We thunder |
| ᎫńǴ | híi | while our teeth |
| ńᏌ | íe | talk. |
| ҺñɢᎠóᏍᏌ | ðiištówe | Take off a garment. |
| ᒼñǴҺō ᏌᎠӑᎫᎴ | mįįáðee ehtáha | At sundown |
| ҺᎴҺᎴ | xáxa | leaflike layers |
| ᏞáᏃᏌ | léže | stipple |
| ᏞñᎠᎴ | níita | the flooding water. |

81

## ᵐáza Ðáðʌ7a / Mą́ze Htáhtaze / Typewriter

| | | |
|---|---|---|
| ᵽʌzázʌȟɒ | pažázaki | I zigzag |
| ᵐázʌ | máza | into the world |
| ʌȟó | wak ó | a woman, |
| ȟóðʌ | šǫ́htą | a wolf. |
| oɕȋ | olį́į̨ | Within my heart |
| ȟʌʌ ʌɛáⱥɒ | hkáwa wahcéxi | an untamed horse, |
| ðȁcȟʌ | tą́ąska | what-do-you-call-it, |
| ðāɛá | htaacé | the wind. |
| ʃoʌȟɴʌ | howąįkíha | Which pathway to |
| ᵐɒȟʌȟ'a | mihkák e | that star |
| ᵐɒȟʌȟ'a ozʌȟa | mihkák e óząke | or the orbit of a star. |
| oᵽ'ȁȟʌ | op ą́ða | Vapor rises off standing water. |
| ʌᵐʌȟɒ | ámąši | Upstairs, |
| ɴⱥoᵽa | íxope | tell untruths, |
| ȟȁ7a | ðéeze | that of a tongue. |
| ȟȁðⱥʌ | ðétxą | Time is just |
| ᵐáza ðáðʌ7a | mą́ze htáhtaze | the ticking noise against metal. |

# Notes

*Epigraph*
Stanza 5 from the Osage "Song Upon the Walking of the Animal Skins." *The Osage and the Invisible World: From the Works of Francis La Flesche* (1995), edited by Garrick A. Bailey.

*Heritage VII*
"Thanks to its status as an endangered species, Osage County infrastructure and drilling projects require a beetle habitat check." From "American Burying Beetle could be reclassified from endangered to threatened" by Lenzy Krehbiel-Burton, *Osage News* (October 2019).

*Heritage VIII*
Refers to the prehistoric remains of the Osage buried in the Clarksville mounds in Missouri.

*Heritage IX*
Origin of the term "Red Skins": ". . . the bodies of Natives brought in for bounty." *Poet Warrior* by Joy Harjo (W.W. Norton, 2021).

*Heritage X*
During the 1920s, because of oil under their land, the Osage were considered one of the wealthiest people in the world. My mother was born in 1925, during the Reign of Terror (1921–1926), a tragic period of American history when outsiders murdered the Osage for their oil headrights.

Lupine *Nocturne*
"The Alaskan lupine arrived in Iceland in 1945 in a suitcase." From "Why Iceland is Turning Purple: Buoyed by Climate Change, an Invasive Plant is Taking Over the Landscape of the Island Nation" by Egill Bjarnason, *Hakai Magazine*, January 16, 2018.

*Ghost Fishing*
The Icelandic myth of Kerling and Karl tells the story of a wife who, while searching for her husband, turns into a boulder when she sees the sun rise. Dritvik Cove, Iceland.

**No** is dedicated to Susan Sommer and Stephen Warnke.

*Kitihawa Speaks*
Kitihawa (Potawatomi), with her husband Jean Baptiste Point Du Sable, established the first permanent settlement in Chicago. The only reference to her life was included in Hugh Heward's "Journal from Detroit to Illinois: 1790." An excerpt: "Monday May 10th 1790 Stopt at Poiint Sables anchord with the cannots & begun to hull Corn & bake Bread & arranged everything for next Morning...."

*In Memoriam*
Excerpted from *The Oklahoman* (Oklahoma City, OK), "findagrave.com." George Bigheart, Pearl's father, was the son of Chief Peter Bigheart and the brother of Eliza Bigheart Tall Chief. Pearl, who was twelve years old when her father was murdered, was raised by her aunt Eliza.

*After* **Killers of the Flower Moon**
I first met Lily Gladstone, who plays Mollie Burkhart, after the Osage Nation premiere of *Killers of the Flower Moon*. My poem, *"Wi'-gi-e"* (*Bestiary*, Red Hen Press, 2009), is spoken in the voice of Mollie Burkhart and includes the line: "During 'Xtha-cka Zhi-ga Tse-the,' the 'Killer of the Flowers Moon.'"

*𐓏𐓘𐓓𐓘𐓓𐓟 / Wahzhazhe / Osage*
"*Wa-zha'-zhe*, name of the Osage tribe... who came from the stars." *The Osage and the Invisible World: From the Works of Francis La Flesche*. The orthography is from the Osage Nation Online Dictionary.

***Peyote Button Necklace*** is dedicated to my cousin, Alexander Tallchief Skibine (1952–2023).

*𐓐𐓂𐓟𐓤𐓘 / Ho'-e-ga / Snare*
The Osage phonetic spelling is from *A Dictionary of the Osage Language* (1932) by Francis La Flesche. "This space they called the *ho'-e-ga*, or snare of life, referring to a snare or trap 'into which all life comes through birth and departs therefrom by death. This space also was called *i-u'-thu-ga* or cavity of

the mouth.'" *The Osage and the Invisible World: From the Works of Francis La Flesche.*

### 𐓷𐓘𐓧𐓟́𐓨𐓘 / *Waléze* / **Stationery**
The phonetic spelling in the middle column is from the *Osage Dictionary* (2009) by Carolyn Quintero.

### 𐓨𐓘́𐓯𐓟 𐓡𐓰𐓘́𐓡𐓯𐓟 / *Mą́ze Htáhtaze* / **Typewriter**
The phonetic spelling in the middle column is from Quintero's *Osage Dictionary*.

With gratitude to Christoper Côté of the Osage Nation Language Department who provided the Osage orthography for "𐓰𐓪́𐓘𐓤𐓘 / *Ho'-e-ga* / Snare," "𐓷𐓘𐓧𐓟́𐓨𐓘 / *Waléze* / Stationery," and "𐓨𐓘́𐓯𐓟 𐓡𐓰𐓘́𐓡𐓯𐓟 / *Mą́ze Htáhtaze* / Typewriter," and for other poems throughout this book.

The Osage Nation Language Department created its own orthography in 2004, revising it between 2012–2014. The Osage Nation claimed back our language by inventing this new thirty-six-character orthography.

# Biographical Note

Author photo by Beowulf Sheehan

Elise Paschen, an enrolled member of the Osage Nation, is the author of *Tallchief, The Nightlife, Bestiary, Infidelities* (winner of the Nicholas Roerich Poetry Prize), and *Houses: Coasts*. As an undergraduate at Harvard, she received the Garrison Medal for poetry. She holds M.Phil. and D.Phil. degrees from Oxford University. Her poems have been published widely, including *Poetry Magazine, The New Yorker, When the Light of the World Was Subdued, Our Songs Came Through: A Norton Anthology of Native Nations Poetry* and *The Best American Poetry*. She is the editor of *The Eloquent Poem* and has edited or co-edited numerous other anthologies, including *The New York Times* bestseller, *Poetry Speaks*. A co-founder of *Poetry in Motion*, Paschen teaches in the MFA Writing Program at the School of the Art Institute of Chicago.

www.ingramcontent.com/pod-product-compliance
Lightning Source LLC
LaVergne TN
LVHW081446310725
817550LV00005B/270